Favorite American Children's Authors

by Kathryn E. Lewis
illustrated by Deborah J. White

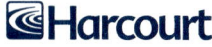

Harcourt
Orlando Boston Dallas Chicago San Diego
Visit *The Learning Site!*
www.harcourtschool.com

Table of Contents

Alma Flor Ada 3
Louisa May Alcott 4
L. Frank Baum 5
Madeleine L'Engle 6
Julius Lester 7
Jack London 8
Dr. Seuss 9
Shel Silverstein 10
Gary Soto 11
Mildred Taylor 12
Yoshiko Uchida 13
E.B. White 14
Laura Ingalls Wilder . . .15
Laurence Yep 16

Introduction

Do you have a favorite book you love to read over and over and over? Each time you open the book and begin to read, are you transported to a familiar place once again? If you have had this experience, you are part of a worldwide community of readers.

In this book, you will meet many beloved American children's authors. Some wrote their stories, poems, or novels over one hundred years ago. Some are still writing as you read these words. Whenever and wherever they sat down to write, these authors all shared the ability and the desire to use words to communicate about our common human experiences.

Alma Flor Ada (1938–)

Alma Flor Ada has lived in Cuba, Spain, Peru, and the United States. The award-winning author of many children's books, Ada is also a professor in San Francisco. There, she directs a center for multicultural education. "Knowing two languages has made the world richer for me," the author once wrote. Because she has such a strong, multicultural vision of the world, Ada is pleased that most of her books have been published in both English and Spanish.

Alma Flor Ada grew up in a "wonderful big old house" in Cuba. Living in a world of fruit trees and animals was a joy for the imaginative young writer. Her grandmother taught her how to read before she was three years old by using a stick to write in the ground the names of plants and flowers.

Alma Flor Ada believes that one reason she became a writer was to communicate some of her childhood pleasures to other children. Many of her books include stories based on experiences from Ada's extraordinary childhood in Cuba.

Louisa May Alcott (1832–1888)

Louisa May Alcott is best known for her novel *Little Women*. Many readers of all ages have enjoyed meeting the four March sisters and learning about their lives in a nineteenth century New England town. Alcott was born on November 29, 1832. When she was two, her family moved to Massachusetts.

In fact, Alcott's childhood home, called Hillside, was also the name of the March family's home in *Little Women*. That house, as well as the house Alcott lived in as an adult, is still open for tours in the town of Concord, Massachusetts.

Alcott wrote her first novel at the age of nineteen, although it was not published for nearly another 150 years! Nevertheless, writing was not Louisa May Alcott's only career. She worked as a teacher and as a seamstress. During the Civil War, Alcott served as a nurse in Washington, D.C. Later, she became an editor of a children's magazine.

Still, writing was her main career, and Alcott worked hard at it. At first, local papers paid her only five dollars for each submitted story. In 1869, after both volumes of *Little Women* were published, Alcott finally received the fame she deserved.

L. Frank Baum (1856–1919)

Nearly forty years before Dorothy, Tin Man, Lion, and Scarecrow appeared on the movie screen, *The Wizard of Oz* was one of the most popular books ever written in this country. The author, L. Frank Baum, was born in a small town in New York State, the fifth of nine children. Because of a weak heart, Baum's childhood was insulated from too much outdoor activity. He became a passionate reader, especially of fiction.

When he was fourteen, Baum started his own writing career by publishing a neighborhood newspaper. As he grew up, no matter what "day job" he had, Baum wrote constantly. During his life, he worked as a salesman, newspaper reporter, theater manager, and store owner, but he was always a writer.

Frank Baum produced many different kinds of writing. In 1881, he wrote a successful play. In 1886, he even wrote a book on raising chickens! Then, in 1900, he published *The Wizard of Oz*, which became an instant best-seller. From then until his death, Baum continued to write about Oz and its magical inhabitants. All in all, he wrote fourteen Oz books, which is why he was called "The Royal Historian of Oz."

Madeleine L'Engle (1918–)

Madeleine L'Engle knew she wanted to become a writer from the time she was five years old. She wrote her first novel in the early 1940s, when she was acting with a small theater group in New York City. Later, while raising three children, L'Engle and her husband opened a general store in rural New England. Still, she kept writing, and in 1962, *A Wrinkle in Time* was published.

A Wrinkle in Time won several awards the year it appeared, and launched L'Engle's career as a writer. In the prize-winning novel, the hero, Meg Austin, risks her life by time-traveling to save her physicist father, who is lost in space. L'Engle wrote several other novels about the adventures of the Austin family.

When the celebrated author was asked what message she hoped children would take from her books, Madeleine L'Engle replied, "Be brave! Have courage! Don't fear!"

Julius Lester (1939–)

As a boy, Julius Lester was not a very good writer. Yet today he is an award-winning author. He has written more than twenty-five books for adults and children, including folktales, novels, poetry, and nonfiction. He has also written more than one hundred essays in magazines and newspapers.

Growing up in Nashville, Tennessee, Julius Lester sang, wrote songs, and played several instruments. He dreamed of becoming a musician, and his first book was actually about guitar playing. After publishing several other books, he decided to write about slavery. His great-grandparents were slaves, and he wrote *To Be a Slave* to help young people understand what that must have been like. "I write," Lester said, "because the lives of all of us are stories. The differences are merely in the details."

Julius Lester did not start out to be a writer, but many thousands of readers are happy that he decided to put his ideas on paper.

Jack London (1876–1916)

Jack London's adventurous life provided the material for some of the most exciting stories in American literature. As a teenager, London sailed the Pacific Ocean on fishing boats and hitched rides around the country on trains. After finally graduating from high school at age twenty-two and spending the next winter in Alaska, he began his career as a writer.

London's Alaskan trip helped him write famous novels such as *The Call of the Wild* and *White Fang.* His later travels led to stories of exotic places such as the South Pacific islands. From the sunsets over tropical islands to the dusty remnants of abandoned mining towns and oil refineries, the details from London's own journeys always found their way into his novels.

London's vivid details offer his readers a chance to feel the warmth of a tropical rainstorm and hear the sounds of howling sled dogs muffled by thickly falling snow. That is why translations of his books are still popular all over the world.

As the author of more than fifty books on many different topics, Jack London was one of the most famous Americans of the early twentieth century.

Dr. Seuss (1904–1991)

As a boy, Theodor Seuss Geisel loved to make his friends laugh. In college, he used his clever wit in cartoons and funny stories, which he often signed with his middle name, Seuss. (Later, while working for a popular humor magazine, he added *Dr.* to his writing name.)

Dr. Seuss began writing for children in 1936. One of his first books, *Horton Hatches an Egg*, features the kind of funny characters that made him the most famous children's writer in America.

After serving in the Army, Dr. Seuss continued to write. In 1954, his publisher asked if he could create a fun book for beginning readers using only 250 simple words. The result was *The Cat in the Hat*, loved by generations of children. A few years later, when a friend challenged him to write a book using only fifty words, he produced *Green Eggs and Ham*, which is one of the most popular books ever written in English.

Although he himself had no children, Dr. Seuss and his books have certainly helped to raise millions of young readers.

Shel Silverstein (1930–1999)

Shel Silverstein started writing as a young boy, and he never stopped. He wrote a movie, several plays, and many hit songs, but he is best known for his children's books. Have you read *Lafcadio: The Lion Who Shot Back* or *The Giving Tree*? What about the poems in *Where the Sidewalk Ends*, *A Light in the Attic*, or *Falling Up*? If you have never read any of Shel Silverstein's writing, get busy. You are in for a treat!

Shel Silverstein wanted his books—whether prose or poetry, wickedly funny or gently serious—to reach people of all ages. His most famous book, in fact, was almost turned down because a well-known publisher thought it would not sell. The publisher was afraid no one would know whether it was a children's book or an adult book. Thirty-five years later, *The Giving Tree* has sold over 5 million copies! Shel Silverstein, who loved to make other people laugh, must have laughed at that himself.

Gary Soto (1952–)

Young writers are often told to "write what you know." Gary Soto knows what it means to grow up in the Mexican American neighborhoods of cities such as Fresno, California, where he was born and raised. In his award-winning stories, essays, and poems, Soto brings these communities to life.

Gary Soto didn't grow up in a wealthy neighborhood. The area where he and his family lived was also home to many factories and old junkyards. What mattered most to Soto, however, were the close relationships he had with friends and family members.

Whether he writes about playing under a sprinkler on a hot summer day or how to deal with a bully or a death in the family, Gary Soto helps readers see that human relationships are what matter to people of all ages. In that way, Soto helps his readers understand that no matter how different their lives may seem, as human beings, they share many common experiences.

Mildred Taylor (1943–)

Although award-winning writer Mildred Taylor grew up in Ohio, her family made yearly visits to Mississippi to visit their extended family in the South. As a child, Taylor saw each trip as "a marvelous adventure, a twenty-four hour picnic that took us into another time and another world." Later, when Taylor became a children's author, she used the rural South of the 1930s as the setting for many of her books, which described the experiences and difficulties of family life for African Americans.

Much of Taylor's love for storytelling came from her father, who often told her stories about their ancestors. Her father's stories were always about ordinary people, but the way in which he told the stories made the people seem heroic to his daughter.

Some of her family's stories made their way into Taylor's writing. Her first novel, *Song of the Trees*, was based on something that happened to a family member. Taylor decided that the best way to tell the story was through the eyes of an eight-year-old narrator, Cassie Logan. Her award-winning novel *Roll of Thunder, Hear My Cry* continues the story of the Logan family.

Yoshiko Uchida (1922–1992)

A teacher as well as a writer, Yoshiko Uchida was born in California and spent much of her life there. During World War II, Uchida, her older sister, and their parents were sent to internment camps along with other Japanese Americans.

Caught in a tragic period in American history, Uchida watched horror-stricken as fear created a partition between the Japanese American community and the rest of the country. In both camps where Uchida and her family were sent, Uchida became a grade-school teacher for the children living in the camps.

In 1952, Yoshiko Uchida received a fellowship, or funding, to study in Japan and research folktales there. One of her books, *Picture Bride*, describes the experiences of many Japanese women arriving in America to be married in the first half of the twentieth century.

In fact, most of Uchida's books focus on the lives of Japanese Americans and the difficulties involved in being part of two cultures. As Uchida wrote, "For although it is important for each of us to cherish our own special heritage, I believe, above everything else, we must all celebrate our common humanity."

E.B. White (1899–1985)

E.B. White loved boats, farm life, animals, and children. As a writer, he found a way to make good use of all these interests.

For many years, White wrote essays and columns for two famous magazines, *Harper's* and *The New Yorker*. These articles were often about life on his farm in Maine.

In 1945, White wrote his first children's book. Called *Stuart Little*, this is the story of a two-inch mouse who is born into a family of humans. Stuart lives life to the fullest, while at the same time fending off the other animal member of the Little family, the prowling family cat, Snowball. For decades, millions of children and adults around the world have loved reading about Stuart's wonderful adventures.

E.B. White wrote two other popular books for children. In *Charlotte's Web*, he created a beautiful story about a lovable pig whose life is saved by a very special spider. In *The Trumpet of the Swan*, White told the story of a young swan who triumphs over a very serious problem.

In all his children's books, E.B. White's characters teach readers how bravery and cleverness can solve many problems. His books are a joy to read—at any age.

Laura Ingalls Wilder (1867–1957)

"I had no idea I was writing history," said Laura Ingalls Wilder, when she realized that her life experiences, as described in her classic eight-volume series of books, were known throughout the world.

Laura Ingalls Wilder was born in Wisconsin in 1867. When she was still a baby, her parents lost all their money and the family became homesteaders in the West. The family lived a rugged pioneer life, moving from place to place. By the time she was fifteen, Laura had become a teacher, and before her twentieth birthday, she had married Almanzo James Wilder, a farmer who had driven her home from school each weekend.

It was not until her daughter urged her to write about her life that Laura Ingalls Wilder began to write her memoirs. Today thousands of visitors tour the sites and places Wilder made famous in her books. "The Wilder Trail" begins in Pepin, Wisconsin (*Little House in the Big Woods*); then heads south to Independence, Kansas (*Little House on the Prairie*); north to Walnut Grove, Minnesota *(On the Banks of Plum Creek);* and west to De Smet, South Dakota (*Little Town on the Prairie*). It is a tour into a lost era in American history.

Laurence Yep (1948–)

As a child in San Francisco, Laurence Yep loved to read science fiction and fantasy books. The first story he ever published, when he was eighteen, was science fiction. The magazine paid Yep one penny for each word!

Since then, Laurence Yep has written many books. These include fantasy, science fiction, history, historical fiction, mysteries, and an autobiography. In many of his stories, Yep uses material from Chinese and Chinese American culture and history. One of his most popular books, *Dragonwings*, is based on Chinese kite flying. Yep learned about making and flying kites from his father, who learned this craft from the old men who lived in San Francisco's Chinatown.

Whatever he is writing about, Laurence Yep says, "Good writing brings out what's special in ordinary things. Writing only requires taking one step to the side and looking at something from a slightly different angle."